THE BEST ADVICE I NEVER GOT

Wisdom for Our Daughters

THE BEST ADVICE I NEVER GOT

Wisdom for Our Daughters

COMPILED BY:
M.E. PORTER

© 2019 Marilyn E Porter

All rights reserved. No portion of this book may be replicated in any form with the express permission of the Publisher and/or the Author or Primary Compiler. Failure to comply with this may result in legal action.

ISBN-13: 978-1-7327340-8-1

Library of Congress Control Number: 2019901620

Publisher:
SBG Media Group, LLC
Dallas, GA

FOREWORD

Teach a youth about the way he should go; even when he/she is old, he will not depart from it.

Proverbs 22:6 (HCSB)

It is the responsibility of the elders, to teach the younger! Without wisdom, they will perish, and the blood will be on the hands of those of us, that knew better. We must stop withholding the truth, as it is designed to leave clues for those coming behind us.

I've gathered a few of the wise ones and set out to begin leaving those clues!

They say success leaves clues - well it our greatest desire that our words, that have been shared from the depth of our hearts, will be the establishment of success – beginning with simply teaching our daughters to make wise choices.

Wisdom and love are a great combination!

Marilyn

PREFACE

I don't quite recall ever feeling like a child, like a little human being who had larger human being to go to for wisdom and guidance. However, I recall moments of confusion and chaos in my young mind. A constant wandering of what things meant that were going on around me. As a mother of 3 girl children myself, it has always been my desire to equip my daughters with real solid, usable wisdom that would erase or at the very least, lessen the confusion in the young mind. I AM A MOTHER! I am not just a mother to the fruit of my own womb, but I am mother to many and to many it is my responsibility to impart that same wisdom and knowledge.

With much prayer I gathered others to join me on this journey to pour into our daughters, my daughters, in hopes that they would receive and apply it to their own lives. The mission of this book is to brand, engrain, emboss and stain their very souls with the message that simply states, "*I am enough*!"

I NEVER GOT

Every young woman needs to know that she is the gift of God – a gift that is not to be disrupted or disturbed in any malicious way. Kindness, gentleness, peace and love are God's desire for His daughters, both your and old but to our baby girls – we **MUST** deliver this message with absolute clarity. Leave nothing to wonder about the value of their very presence on this planet.

Daughters,
You are amazingly and strikingly beautiful. Your uniqueness is a that of a designer original; no other person the earth has your fingerprint- YOU ARE DIVINE! And if no other ever tells this, please hide this in your heart, "God is with you and HE has fashioned a planned so splendid plan for your life that cannot be stopped by anyone! You are here for all of this!

Much Love and Many Blessings,
Your Village

ACKNOWLEDGEMENTS

To my Co-Creators of this phenomenal literary work I honor your gift of words and wisdom.

DEDICATION

*Misha,
Christina,
Charity.*

My One heart for My Three loves.

TABLE OF CONTENTS

PREFACE
FOREWORD
ACKNOWLEDGEMENTS
DEDICATIONS

1. L. CHANEL THOMPSON   13

2. ANGELA MOUNTZ   27

3. CRISTIN GERMAINE   38

4. MICHELLE EDELEN JONES   54

5. SHAWNEE PENKACIK   68

6. FRED "FUNKI" MILLS   82

7. CELETHA RILEY   90

8. CHOU HALLEGRA   104

9. ALMENA L. MAYES   118

10.   TOSHA DEARBONE   127

11.   MARILYN E. PORTER   139

I NEVER GOT

…

For our Daughters

L. CHANEL THOMPSON

L. Chanel channels her infectious energy, jovial spirit, and positive life outlook into empowering others to "heal the hurt", recognize their potential and take bold action to identify and achieve their life's PURPOSE. With professional expertise in writing, teaching, training and project management she is primed to bring all her resources together to share guidance to young women and men, coupling her special mastery for program development with successfully navigating life FREE from DRAMA.

L. Chanel is a preacher, the author of The Drama Free Blueprint: Keys to Coming Straight Outta Drama – The Drama FREE Architect TM, a certified family mediator and co-parenting coach –The Blended Family Strategist TM.

She is following a God-given mandate to make the Bible a relevant 21st century force for the right now, "microwave" "millennial" generation by "preaching to the streets". She is also a "MOMpreneur" with several businesses in motion through L. Chanel Ink TM. Although she absolutely loves writing, fashion, shopping and traveling, her most important jobs are simply Wife, Mother and Minister to Whomever the Lord allow.

I DEDICATE

This is dedicated to my mother, Sylvia, the perfectly purposed mother that I needed, I love you with all that is within me.

To all the daughters that I've had the honor to mother

To my unborn daughter.

1. You Are MORE Than Smart

Advice is an interesting thing because it's often unsolicited. More often than that, it's inapplicable because situations are so significantly unique that we truly must have the wisdom of God and the leading of the Holy Spirit above all else to navigate life; and yet, here I am – advising my unborn daughter and daughters everywhere, including the daughter that I used to be.

But this not the kind of advice that one gives without purpose or with mal-intent. This is advice that comes from a place of deep introspection and healing, of pain and perseverance. It's an exposition on the process that it takes to BECOME. My earnest prayer is that what I was not given, that I may give, that it may bless someone else; that what I went through as my purpose

process would bless someone else to go through their own purpose process. That what I testify to will do as the Holy Bible says – help someone to **OVERCOME**. It's really an intercessory
prayer for those coming into their own understanding about who they are and who they are destined to be. It's something that I never got because I was raised in a family where they didn't know that sharing and telling what happened to them was power and life and help to those who would come after them, but I broke that silent killer curse!

This is, "The Best Advice that I Never Got", my prayer, and my open letter to my unborn daughter.

Dearest Princess,

There I was, standing in the podium of the St. Matthew Lutheran Church - a 14-year-old eighth grader, soon to be high schooler - one of two salutatorians of the graduating class. I had been mocked because there were two of us, as if I had not earned every "A". As if I had not done every assignment with my best ability. As if I had not proven myself worthy to be there. They said I had cried to my teacher AND my principal AND my assistant principal for them to allow me to be one of two of the top three in my graduating class.

The thought! AND I was innocent of every charge. I had done none of it. Little did they know, well, little did I know if we're telling the truth, that scholarship was a GIFT that I had not asked for any more than being a salutatorian. I mean, really? If all I had to do was cry and plead, would I not plead for the number one spot as valedictorian! The thought! AND I decided that I would never be accused of such craziness again. I would somehow escape these lying tongues and jealous hearts. I would escape to high school with a fresh start and never see or hear from these people again.

That's my first piece of advice, my dearest princess:

Don't make ultimatums with your destiny.
You are who you are and there's nothing anyone can do about it, but your mother has learned some things and so you will be able to talk to me about it. I will freely talk to you about it. You are who you are and there will be people who hate you for it and there's nothing you can do about it. You cannot outrun your purpose, you cannot avoid your destiny and you cannot escape
the hate. It's part of the purpose and plan of God. Just trust in Psalm 23 like your mother did; the Word of God cannot fail.

I NEVER GOT

I'll never forget writing that first "speech". It was handwritten, and it was messy – it went against all my perfectionist ways – I remember the freedom I felt when I wrote the words and power that came over me when I spoke those words. The overwhelming emotion evoked and the feeling of being exactly where I was supposed to be. That was the first time I felt purposed and yet I had no one to affirm me, to push me, to pray for me, or help me with my process and so I fell into the depths of pain and promiscuity instead. I had a gaping hole in my soul, and I tried to fill it with boys because I thought that sex equaled intimacy and love. And let's be clear – it can mean those things – but not outside of a God-ordained marriage. The hole was a "Father sized hole" that had been strategically placed there by God Himself. Did you hear me? Our Heavenly Father placed a Father sized HOLE in me that only He could fill to make me WHOLE! I felt the hole, but no one ever told me how to fill the hole.

That's my second piece of advice my beloved princess:
No matter what, see everything that happens or fails to happen to you as part of your purpose.

THE BEST ADVICE

I didn't have an Earthly father to love on me and tell me I was a princess. I didn't have an Earthly father to put me on a public pedestal for all to see. My Earthly father kept me a secret because of his own personal shame. And yet, I freely tell it! Not only do I tell it freely, but I was able to stand in the purpose of breaking the generational curse of having children out of wedlock AND creating a legacy of marriage and fatherhood. You see how God did that? I've already told you that you have a destiny and you don't have to make deals about it and Jeremiah 29:11 is your proof - I am the witness. The very fact that as I write this, you are not born and that I know you will be born is further proof.

Now I'm telling you that you have a purpose. It's specific to YOU. Indeed, I prayed for you and your brothers and God has honored His promises, but even distinct from your promised purpose to me – you are purposed by God. You don't need the affirmations of people, not even your parents, because people may not give you what you think you need, but you need to believe what God has said about you above all. What God shows you in visions and dreams is real. What God reveals to you deep down inside is real. What God gives you as gifts, is your affirmation.

I was gifted with scholarship – I don't ever remember having to study or having difficulty in school, except that Chemistry Regents and that PMP exam! Those were epic "fails", but they taught me that what God wants me to do, will be revealed in the ease in which I achieve it.

Those are what I believe are ordered steps. Writing is also a gift. I do it with pleasure and ease.

Speaking is also a gift. I do it with power, precision and passion. These are also the areas where

I am effective with others. Do you see how your gifts tie into your purpose and lead you to your destiny? I remember the Lord telling me, "Lead with the Gifts", and I've strived to do so ever since. My prayer is that you will do the same.

You are MORE than SMART, you are SPECIAL. *The entire Holy Bible is a series of books written to tell you how special you are. How you are a spirit and you were created to have an Earthly assignment – your destiny – and you have a specific assignment – your purpose – and you have everything you need to accomplish it. You are smart, you have been naturally gifted and your gifts make it seem easy. But you are also special to God and He has created a place for you on the Earth to have dominion. You will be the best at it because only you are purposed to*

THE BEST ADVICE

do it. Don't ever shy away from being the best at being YOU.

That's the third piece of advice my sweet, special princess:

BE YOU.

Don't ever compromise YOU for what others want you to be, not even me, your mother. Trust me, I did that and did nothing but waste precious time trying to live up to your grandmother's expectations – another epic "fail". You be every single bit of YOU and don't ever feel the need to compare yourself to anyone, not even me. I know it will be challenging because the world thrives off comparison and competition, but there's a scripture for that too! Exodus 20:17, I refer to it as Commandment Number 10, tells us not to covet anything anyone else has and it's one that is so easy to break, even in the private spaces of your heart and mind. But know that God is no respecter of any person and just like that Jeremiah Scripture says, God knew you BEFORE you were formed in the womb, and so you must fight to stay focused on the reason YOU are here. You will know the truth of your birth. I will not lie to you. You will know the truth of your lineage. I will not lie to you. I will give you what was not given to me – the TRUTH – and you will be made free so that you can soar like an eagle.

It took me 25 years to gather information, fill in the blanks and then accept it all. It took me 25 years to fulfill the prophecy that my mother said over me in her belly. It took me 25 years to receive Jesus Christ into my heart even though I always had God in my head, because it was about more than being smart. All those religion classes gave me the structure and the discipline, but I needed the last piece to the puzzle – the SPIRIT.

And that is my next piece of advice my promised purposed princess:
Don't let anyone or anything steer you from the knowledge and truth of Jesus, the Christ. There will be intricately weaved stories. There will be false signs and there will be false prophets. These things are not new. They are the same tricks of old and they cannot work.
Jesus is the Savior and He is the ONLY way to successfully navigate in life and obtain eternal life. No matter what, let this mind be in you that was in Christ Jesus! Let the fact that John 3:16 is the TRUTH remain in your mind and in your heart. God loves YOU. Period. God sent His only begotten Son, Jesus, into the world just for YOU. You need only to believe that fact and

every truth will be known to you. The reason that this advice is so important is because of the final piece of advice.

People, even those who truly love you will tell you that you are "smart", but they will rarely tell you that you are "special". Because telling you that you are special, to most people, leaves them feeling inadequately special as if telling you about your specific special somehow takes away from their specific special. **So, here's my final piece of advice my purposed princess:**
Own your specific special.
Don't take a long time either. Own it early and earnestly. People will get over it or they'll get out of your way. God has a strategic way of moving you or them to get His divine will accomplished. Remember, my first piece of advice. Even if no one ever tells you that you are special – you have these words. "YOU ARE SPECIAL. YOU ARE UNIQUE. YOU WILL DO GREAT THINGS BECAUSE YOU HAVE A PURPOSE TO DO SO." Why do you need this?
Because life is a challenge that tests your purpose. Life perfects your purpose like gold refinery. Life is your litmus test for your testimony to the goodness, the greatness and the grace of God.

Don't be fooled by the "successful", but instead, always strive to be spiritual. Therein, is your special sanctuary of power and freedom - 2 Corinthians 3:17 is your proof of that. You are FREE, if you operate in the spirit of Christ. Tap into it often. Do not be afraid to be alone with you and God. Alone is where you are anointed, appointed and affirmed to do the great things of your purpose!

Now, I'm not going to leave you with this advice without a commitment. Be careful of those who are quick to give advice; but leave you without commitment about the advice. If I live, I will lead you and guide you with the wisdom of Christ. I am committed to do what the Holy Bible instructs a parent to do in Proverbs 22:6, "Train up a child in the way that s/he should go and when they are old, s/he will not depart from it". That's the part of this prayer, this letter, this advice that is most important, because it's the reason why I'm praying, writing and advising in the first place. Let the wisdom that I've obtained, the truth that has been revealed to me, now enlighten you, sweet, smart, special purposed princess. **You Are Unstoppable!**
Amen.
Sincerely,
Mother

THE BEST ADVICE

You

are not a mistake

 **ANGELA MOUNTZ** has been around a few blocks in her life. Growing up in an abusive home where alcoholism and drugs were prevalent, she decided she would travel down a different path. That path included some addiction issues herself, a failed marriage and most recently a heroin addicted child. But through it all she seeks her identity in God and finds joy in the little things. She has a pastoral license from the Brethren in Christ and a social science degree specializing in Families and Children. Her passions include identity in Christ, healing from woundedness and loving people where they are at. God has given her a second chance with an amazing man she has been married to for 7 years. Together they live in central PA with their 4 delightful cats.

2. True Sight

As little girls we learn that we need approval: The television tells us we must always be ready, dressed to impress and you should never let them see you sweat. The list goes on and on.

As 42-year-old women you would think that reflecting the advice I would give was to ignore the nonsense that the proverbial they tell us but it's not. I appreciate the opinion of a good friend, I do always want to be ready and being sweaty outside of the gym isn't on my list of things to do. The advice that I would give and what I would like my daughters, nieces and the women in my life to know is that your body is a temple that was created by God. God alone defines who you are, and you should treat that temple as a precious gift.

Sounds like a Disney cliché, right? It really isn't. The concept of letting your creator define you will save you from much heartache in this fallen world. Let's break down this temple and the gift from God. The first thing we need to remember is that the temple of our body isn't just the physical body. It's the many layers of who we are and what makes up the unique person that you are. This temple is comprised of many layers.

The first layer is the outside shell. This is your skin, your hair, your eyes. Your skin is considered the largest organ of our bodies. The earth's environment is harsh, and the sun, wind and rain damage the gift of protection that your body's skin gives you. My earliest memories of my mother were her hands. My mother grew up in a generation where sunscreen was not a requirement. She also lived during the time when the baked look was cool. Her hands were the first to age. I look at my hands today and I see my mom's hands. The beginning of arthritis causing my knuckles to swell and the telltale signs of age lines making sure that I know that time marches on. I remember looking at my mom during her last days and not being able to recognize her. The ravages of life made her skin look old beyond her years. We need to remember that our physical bodies are the temple. And you and I are the brides. When we begin to view ourselves in this manner, we begin to recognize the importance of the temple. Think for a moment of your most prized physical possession. For me it is my grandmother's dishes. I was blessed by my aunts to receive them as a gift in memory of my grandmother. They hold a special place not only in my heart but in my house. They are protected from breakage and kept out of reach. When I do use them, they are treated with the utmost of care, deliberately washed and put away. I can imagine that when God formed each one of us that He carefully designed our bodies. He made them strong and able. He gave us muscle and bone that work together to move us around and he gave us skin to protect the muscles and bone. How are you treating this temple? Are you respecting the skin, you live in? Arc you nourishing it and protecting it?

The second layer is your muscle's, bones and organs. Did you know that God created the different systems in our bodies to harmonize with each other? And they were created to not only to work well together but to support each other. As with the outer layer we live in a world that encourages eating fast food, drinking in excess and keeping up with everybody else at a fast pace. What God wants from us is for us to exercise our bodies, He wants us to fill it with good food that nourishes our minds and fills our cells with energy and strength. And most importantly He doesn't want us to poison our bodies with substances the world tells us will make us prettier, more appealing and more fun. And the most important layer is your heart, brain and soul. This is where the Holy Spirit lives. I want us to remember Eve in the garden. The serpent used his silver tongue to make Eve doubt herself and to doubt God. He confused her thoughts so that she did the one thing that God told her not to. Had Eve continued to focus on the love of the Father instead of allowing herself to believe lies we may be living a different life right now. This still happens today. The world whispers in our ear telling us that God isn't the measure of our worth. We are told we need to give into our lust and desires and live for the moment.

But that moment has eternal consequences. When we live for moments without thinking of the eternal consequences, we give up pieces of our soul to the enemy. And we cannot get them back. God can and will forgive us, but we cannot turn back time. And what I want for you is to not go through the pain and the shame that goes with disregarding your value. I did not live according to these words for most of my 20's. I lived for my own self and my own desires and I sought to fill the void in my life with worldly band aids. Today I am a redeemed child of God, but I still have a past and I still have scars from those days. I praise the Lord that God loved and still loves me more than I loved myself.

When we define who we are and treat our bodies, souls and minds accordingly we begin a positive pattern of self-care, self-esteem and open ourselves up to living a life creates harmony among our mind, body and soul. A life that is deeply connected to God and will lead to deep connections with others. These connections will be void of abuse, humiliation and shame.

We can do this is three steps;

❖ The first thing we do is believe we are created by the one true God and that He alone matters.

> Despite previous life choices we may have made the reality is that the blood of Christ covers us. Jesus Christ went to the cross so that we could be redeemed. But you need to believe you are worthy!

❖ Second, we need to allow God to root out any negative attitudes and behaviors we may have that do not honor Him or the creation He has made. This is often a slow process. It may mean that we seek physical health or emotional health. It will always mean that we search out the will of God in our lives.

❖ And finally, we need to put it into practice. The world will continue to tell you that you are not worthy, that you should just give in. After all everybody is doing it. But you are a princess of the one true King. You were fearfully and wonderfully made. Go out and let your sparkle shine.

You

are divinely and

uniquely created.

CRISTIN GERMAINE

Single Mom of a 15-year-old son. Cristin works full time in the Health Insurance Industry. She is also the Director of *H.O.P.E* – a Single Moms Ministry established in February of 2013. In 2016, Cristin created a one-day event called, *The Lancaster Dare to Dream Single Moms Day Out*! In 2018, Cristin along with 30 women from around the world co-authored *"The Beauty in My Mess"* – an anthology book comprised of powerful and inspiring stories! Most recently Cristin co-wrote a song based on her life with a Nashville Music Producer being released in early 2019.

I DEDICATE

I dedicate this chapter to the reader. I pray it will encourage you to invest in yourself – because **you** are worth it!

3. THE VILLAGE SUPPORTS YOU

Growing up my life was, let's say... less than ideal. I lived in a dysfunctional home where my parents divorced when I was 3 years old; after which my Mom got together with my step-father who sexually abused me.

Starting out my young life was not a good situation and unfortunately due to these traumatic circumstances I never learned boundaries, or what my value was because it was mixed up in trying to survive this place I called, "home."

It didn't stop there as later in my 20's I married a man who I thought was my Prince Charming, however, he turned out to be abusive – physically, mentally and emotionally. I'm a statistic of domestic violence and one time was beat up very badly. In my marriage I lived in fear, having to walk on eggshells, wondering when the next time I would say the wrong thing, or act in a manner my husband didn't like and pay the consequences of what he thought was inappropriate.

When my son was 3 years old, I secretly planned my getaway out of my abusive relationship. I am now divorced and a single Mom of a 15-year-old son. I share all of this to help you avoid the pitfalls I ended up in, praying that you will never have to experience.

We should feel safe, especially in our homes. When feelings of security are compromised by toxic people, even if they are our family, we are sure to have self-esteem issues and not realize our worth because we are trying to survive in a less than ideal atmosphere.

By age 3, parents should be teaching their children how to deal with certain emotions and how to regulate those emotions. When our parents can't understand their own value, it's hard to teach their children, unfortunately this creates an unhealthy environment in the home.

In their book, "The Whole-Brain Child," Dr. Daniel J. Siegel and Tina Payne Bryson, Ph.D. write, "As children develop, their brains 'mirror' their parent's brain. In other words, the parent's own growth and development, or lack of those, impact the child's brain. As parents become more aware and emotionally healthy, their children reap the rewards and move toward health as well."

Why am I talking about these tragic circumstances, let alone being a toddler? My goal is to help you learn lessons from my past to help you realize how your past will define the decisions you make in your future and have a direct impact on who you are and where you are headed.

By the time I was married, unfortunately I had not learned my worth and value, or how to tell a toxic man from a healthy one because I did not have a good role model of healthy love, and relationships or anyone teaching me about my self-worth.

I'd love to offer you some helpful tips and advice that I wish someone had shared with me, ways to avoid the heartache I've lived through. If you can establish these habits now, it will help you throughout your lifetime and you'll be a healthy-minded individual.

Below are areas I recommend using to establish a safe environment in order to heal, grow and thrive!

Create a Support Network

I NEVER GOT

If you are growing up in the type of environment I was, it will be important for you to find safe people. Do you have friends who you feel comfortable and can be yourself? When you tell them your secrets do, they keep them between the two of you? Do you feel comfortable with their parents and sharing with them, more than your own parents? If you have a good feeling about people and they've proved themselves to keep your secrets, trust your inner feeling that these would be safe people.

When I was going through tough times, I had a handful of trusted friends that I would ask to pray for me, I would send an email to share what was going on and they would immediately start praying and encourage me. Currently, I have a secret Facebook page with people who love and care about me, who any time I have a challenge in my life I post it and they will pray. It's another way to communicate in a quick and easy way and helps relieve my stress.

One of my best pieces of advice for you is to talk, talk, talk – get feelings out, most importantly don't bottle them up. One of Satan's tactics is to keep us shut up, bound up and in a corner feeling lonely, lying to us making us think no one understands. Friends in our lives who love and care about us want to help, but they

THE BEST ADVICE

won't know how until we have the courage to share. Talking is crucial if circumstances are harmful to your well-being. You need to create this safe space - this is another way to do that.

Journal and Write or Draw Your Feelings

Get a journal to write out or draw your feelings. Journaling helps get the yucky feelings out and not keep them bottled up. It's been proven that keeping feelings inside has detrimental effects to our health and relationships. When we get feelings out, we feel better and our friends and family will thank us because we give them a gift of being free of rotten feelings and emotions that we may tend to spew out on them.

Find A Counselor

When I was 13 years old and it was exposed that I had been sexually abused, adults in my life wanted me to get counseling, I HATED IT – Hated that I felt like there was something wrong with me because of someone else's actions!

I didn't want to deal with what was happening because I was still living in the mess that was at home and I was angry. When I moved away to college, I determined that I did not want to grow up to be a bitter person and decided that counseling was a good option. I had to admit that I needed help navigating through all these yucky feelings inside of me.

If you're not at a point to find a counselor, I want to recommend a few helpful books that I read, you can check with your local library.

The first is called, "Safe People," by Henry Cloud and John Townsend. Here's a short description: "They offer solid guidance for making safe choices in relationships, from friendships to romance. They help identify the nurturing people we all need in our lives, as well as ones we need to learn to avoid. Safe People will help you to recognize 20 traits of relationally untrustworthy people. Discover what makes some people relationally safe, and how to avoid unhealthy entanglements. You'll learn about things within yourself that jeopardize your relational security. And you'll find out what to do and what not to do to develop a balanced, healthy approach to relationships."

Another book I found super helpful is, "Boundaries," by Henry Cloud and John Townsend. A description states, "Having clear boundaries is essential to a healthy, balanced lifestyle. A boundary is a personal property line that marks those things for which we are responsible. In other words, boundaries define who we are and who we are not. Boundaries impact all areas of our lives: Physical boundaries help us determine who may touch us and under what circumstances -- Mental boundaries give us the freedom to have our own thoughts and opinions -- Emotional boundaries help us to deal with our own emotions and disengage from the harmful, manipulative emotions of others -- Spiritual boundaries help us to distinguish God's will from our own and give us renewed awe for our Creator."

Thirdly, there is a great website to check out: www.newlife.com, it's a fantastic resource where they can pray with and head you in the direction of a trained counselor, who is highly recommended.

Love Yourself and Who You Are

In Mark 12:28-31, Jesus talks about The Greatest Commandment, "One of the teachers of the law came and heard them debating. Noticing that Jesus had given them a good answer, he asked him, "Of all the commandments, which is the most important?" "The most important one," answered Jesus, "is this: 'Hear, O Israel: The Lord our God, the Lord is one. Love the Lord your God with all your heart and with all your soul and with all your mind and with all your strength.' The second is this: 'Love your neighbor as yourself.' There is no commandment greater than these."

You may be thinking, "OK, so it's a Bible verse, what in the world does this mean for me?" A few years ago, it hit me like a load of bricks where Jesus says, "Love your neighbor as yourself." After reading this passage, it occurred to me, the only way we can love our neighbor is if we love ourselves. That was life-impacting that day because we are constantly being told to be about others best interests, make others feel important, when, the only way you will truly be able to love others is if you love YOURSELF.

Does loving yourself mean that you become selfish and have the attitude, "it's all about me." Not at all, but in order to love yourself you need to learn to care for yourself. Meaning taking time to spend on you, reading good books, praying, reflecting on God's word and allowing the Lord to show you who you are in Him.

Trust me in this, learn to love yourself - YOU are worth investing in!

Forgive Others and Yourself
Want to know a secret? One of the things that will make you a U-G-L-Y girl is un-forgiveness, not only will it show on your face, but it will poison your outlook. Forgiving someone doesn't mean what they did is OK,

it's a way to free yourself from the bondage of never getting past your past. Don't let another person steal your beauty, joy or freedom... forgive and walk in forgiveness every day.

Having been sexually abused by my step-father I didn't want to forgive, but I did, and it was freedom for my soul. As an adult I can live with no regrets, it feels good and my conscience is clear.

Forgive yourself too. Don't be so hard on yourself, if you messed up, forgive yourself and move on. Whatever you did is not worth getting distracted, walk in freedom, and let yourself off the hook.

Do YOU!

It's important and I mean SO IMPORTANT that you do YOU. Unfortunately, as an adult I lost myself in my marriage so when I got divorced, I was in a rut, I didn't know who I was or what I liked, it was a sad, sad story.

If you currently don't like yourself, start on a new journey to find out who you are. What do you like? Where do you like to go? Take personality assessments to learn more about your personality. Take a few months and focus on who you are. Not only will it make you feel good about yourself, but it will make you realize

I NEVER GOT

how uniquely you were created, and the world needs your unique gifts, talents and abilities.

It really all starts with YOU working on YOU!

I want to encourage you to do the hard work it takes developing your character – this is the secret to any healthy relationship – you will attract what you are. If you don't know yourself, your worth and your value - you will attract the wrong kind of relationships. You want to avoid the pain and heartbreak that some of us older, wiser women have faced.

When I was a teenager, I never dated a lot, that can be good, but it can also be bad. Had I learned who I was I most likely wouldn't have settled for being treated so badly by my husband, and I also would have been able to see the red flags in the most important relationship you'll ever have – with your future spouse.

Taking time to work through the above steps, you will avoid getting involved with the wrong relationships. After my divorce I started dating to find out what it as all about since I didn't date in high school, here are some of the best lessons I learned from my adventures:

THE BEST ADVICE

- **If a guy seems too perfect, that IS the red flag**. No one is perfect, we all have flaws, and as much as we work on ourselves, we are imperfect and will never arrive at perfection. I'm not saying look for the imperfections in every guy you date but know that no one guy is perfect. I read once if a guy has 80% of what you're looking for, that's Good... meaning that no person will meet 100% of your criteria.

- **It's true, how a guy treats his Mom reflects how he will treat you**. If a guy is respectful to his Mom, you can bet he will know how to treat you and his Mom will not allow her son to disrespect you either. Respect is a huge foundation of any relationship.

- **A guy will make time to spend with you if he's interested**. Don't waste your time on a guy who is in and out, leaving you questioning if he likes you – this guy is a game player and girl you don't have time for that nonsense. The right guy will give you the attention you deserve.

- **If a guy disrespects you, run, RUN FAR AWAY as quickly as possible**. If the guy you're dating isn't kind, encouraging and loving, once you get married it will only get worse. You want to set the standard high now because you're worth it, make him work for your attention.

- **There are ALWAYS other fish in the sea.** Don't fall for the trap that no one else will love you, there is ALWAYS someone else. It may take time to meet the right guy for you... believe me there are better fish out there, be selective!

- **Any relationship should make your life better.** If a guy has drama and issues going on, walk away, he will try to drag you into his scene. If you're working on you, investing in who you are, you don't have time for drama that drags you down.

Those are my top six picks of the most valuable lessons I learned through dating.

Know this - YOU are worth far more than you may feel. Don't fall into the trap feeling everyone else is better, prettier and more interesting. If I could go back to where you sit right now, I'd want to start by saying your circumstances don't define your worth, you were created for more than this!

Do the hard work.

THE BEST ADVICE

Love yourself.

Pursue your dreams.

You my sweet girl, are worth it!

You

are a gift!

MICHELLE EDELEN JONES

lives by Psalm 34:1, which says, "I will bless The Lord at all times and his praise shall continually be in my mouth." In the good times, Co-Pastor Edelen praises. In the bad times, she also praises. She serves as Co-Pastor along with her husband Elder Timothy R. Edelen of Fountain of Living Waters Church. Michelle is the loving mother to Timothy, Trinity and Timon and grandmother to Bryson.

She is a graduate of North Carolina State University and Meredith College receiving BS in Economics and Business Management and holds as MBA.

Michelle is a Policy Advisor for Community Affairs at the Division of Mental Health, Developmental Disabilities and Substance Abuse Services where she has responsibility for writing public policy related to cultural competency, diversity and inclusion. she is also the CEO of Excellence in All Consulting, where she serves women who need to get to the other side of stuck which is EXCELLENCE, as a Christian life coach, transformational speaker, corporate and ministry trainer.

Michelle is the published author of Getting to Your Place of Excellence: A 10-Day Devotional.

In late 2018, Michelle expanded her business model to include building a team of skincare consultants to support her Rodan+Fields skincare business.

As a speaker, she speaks in numerous venues including schools, corporations, government and non-profit organizations, conferences, and churches. Michelle strives to offer a speaking experience that is inspirational, dynamic, and unforgettable for her audiences. Her mission is simple:

Guide audiences to their *"Place of Excellence."*

Michelle is The Excellence Engineer and is poised and ready to be your personal transformation architect. So, fasten your seatbelt, and get ready for the journey of a lifetime as she gets you to your *Place of Excellence.*

I DEDICATE

It is with great admiration and love that I dedicate this chapter to my first role models, Deacon Emeritus Welton Jones and Dr. Lillie D. Jones. I love you!

I NEVER GOT

4. Life Comes at you F.A.S.T. – BE Ready

I'm reminded of the child's game *Hide N Seek*. As the child who was chosen to find everyone proceeded to count to 10, all the other children ran to hide. After the counter got to 10, they would declare…

"Ready or Not, Here I Come."

Each child sought out that perfect hiding space. The object was to not be found. While the counter was searching for the players, the players were trying get back to home base without being tagged.

From the time the counter declared, "ready or not, here I come, it was an all-out battle to not be found. Everyone found the most obscure place possible to hide. When each child found their prime hiding spot, they knew silence was golden. You see, the counter was not only looking for hiders, he/she was listening for hiders as well. Something as simple as a sneeze could give you away – leading to you being found and tagged out.

Don't you wish life was as simple as this child's game. Think about it. What if you could just hide from life's

THE BEST ADVICE

turmoil? What if you could run back to home base and be safe from the cares and concerns of life? What if you could just say, I'm not ready and the game – life – would stop? If it were all that simple, everyone would master life and live in total abundance.

Well, life is not that simple. You see, some things are simple. Some things are complicated and then some things are complex. For example, baking a cake is simple. You read the instructions on the recipe and follow them step-by-step and then you will have a cake. Now, whether it is ready to win a blue ribbon for best cake or even edible for that matter, you will have a cake. However, flying an airplane is complicated. You must study various manuals, log many practice flight hours, pass several tests and then complete a solo flight (all without crashing) to get your license.

Life, on the other hand, is complex. It is complex because it comes at you F.A.S.T. Complex is a whole made up of complicated or interrelated parts. Things that are complex are difficult to analyze, separate and solve. There parts are confusingly interrelated which are virtually impossible to grasp them separately. They are intricately woven together and can appear to offer disorder. In other words, the complexities of life are hard to explain and understand sometimes.

I NEVER GOT

That gets me to the best advice I never got, Life Comes at you F.A.S.T. (Whether You're Ready or Not). Life doesn't wait for you to get ready. It doesn't even care if you're ready. It will come and no matter what. I remember at a very young age experiencing life coming at me very F.A.S.T. I didn't understand at the time but what I did know is that it would not stop.

I'm reminded of a story my mother often tells about a conversation we had. I was in middle school. I came home from school that day and I asked her if the world could stop so I could get off. She asked what was going on and why would I want to get off the world. I began to explain all the complexities of my middle-school life. This teacher was too mean. This class was too hard. This boy didn't like me. This group of girls didn't want to be my friend. It all seems so simple now but at the time, let's just say it was major! What it was is complex. It was a complex array of confusingly interrelated parts that my maturity level and hormones could not navigate. It was life coming at me F.A.S.T.

By the time I hit high school, I realized in no uncertain terms that life was an ever-evolving ball of pieces and parts that would come together and roll you over if you were not on, you're A-game. That's about the time I realized that life came at you F.A.S.T. and I began to identify what it really meant and was doing to me.

Ferocious – Very fierce or violent

Attitude – A feeling that affects behavior

Stress – A feeling of worry or overwhelming anxiety

Temperamental – Tending to change mood in an unreasonable way

The complexity of life was a feeling for me. It felt ferocious at times because the speed with which life came and smacked me in the face seemed almost violent. I'd go from being perfectly okay to experiencing this fierce attack of things that I could not understand, describe or articulate.

Life seemed attitudinal to me. Now let's face it...I was an attitudinal teenage girl so some of it could have been me. I was certain of this one thing though. Life could easily have affected my behavior. The only reason it didn't is because of my parents. They did not play! For a while, our house was Grand Central Station. Everyone who came through our home quickly came to understand that there were a few non-negotiables. They were:

> You will not live here and do nothing.

> You will be respectful and responsible.

You will pursue whatever is the next level of education for you.

You will do your part to keep the house clean and functioning.

Once these rules were made clear, everyone fell in line. So, as you can see, attitude was not tolerated in my house although life could have brought it out.

The stress of life appeared never ending. It was current as the breath you just took. It was as close as the skin on your body. It was as real as the very essence of who you are. Stress, if unchecked, caused a multitude of issues in your life. Worry and overwhelm were far too common place back then in my life. The things I stressed over then seem so insignificant now but boy oh boy, were they major issues then.

And finally, life was as temperamental as any teenager you've ever met. The mood changes brought on by life were sometimes unbearable. At a minimum, they were neither fun nor beneficial. If left to my own devices, I would have succumbed to my temperamental nature and swung in the direction of whatever was the most current wind blowing. But again, my parents did not play.

So, if life says, *"Ready or Not, Here I Come."* then proceeds to come at you F.A.S.T., your only response is to redefine F.A.S.T. How F.A.S.T. life comes at you will not change. That one thing is constant. What is not constant is where you are in life's struggles. What is not constant is your state of development and growth.

Here again is a point where I must thank my parents. Although they did not give me this advice directly, they equipped me to handle whatever came and however it came. They used the word of God and its principles to shape and guide me. They used the tenets of our faith to help me understand that I didn't just have to accept what came my way but that I had the ability, no the authority to change it. This revelation led to New World Order for me!

I had a total shift in my approach to life. I began to view life the way God wanted me too. I saw life as his way of blessing and prospering me. I no longer saw life as a serious of temptations, tests and trials. I no longer viewed my life as a ferocious, attitudinal, stressful and temperamental mess. I began to see life in a whole new way. F.A.S.T. took on an entirely different meaning.

Faith – Belief, trust and loyalty to God

Anointing – An expression of the sanctifying influence of the Holy Spirit

Sanctification – The process of being made holy and set apart

Time – A continuum of events measured from the past to the future

This new acknowledgment of my ability to define and control F.A.S.T. shifted my life in so many ways. My life changed as my faith began to grow when I came to understand the authority that comes with an increased faith.

To you, O GOD, belong the greatness and the might, the glory, the victory, the majesty, the splendor; Yes! Everything in heaven, everything on earth; the kingdom all yours! You've raised yourself high over all. Riches and glory come from you, you are ruler over all; You hold strength and power in the palm of your hand to build up and strengthen all.

1 Chronicles 29:11-12 (MSG)

This passage was total freedom for me. It helped me understand that I didn't have to lie down and let life do to me whatever it chose. I could stand and be ready as life shot its best shot. I also learned that I was only going to be ready for whatever life threw my way because of God's word and my faith. What a glorious revelation to have.

Next, I replaced attitude with the anointing. I learned early on that Isaiah 10:27 is beyond true. It says,

"And it shall come to pass in that day, that his burden shall be taken away from off thy shoulder, and his yoke from off thy neck, and the yoke shall be destroyed because of the anointing."

You see, allowing life to dictate my attitude was a burden or a yoke around my neck. It was a bondage that was holding me back. I had to come to understand that the anointing is what was needed in my life to combat the power of attitude. Again, another revelation that set me free.

This step in redefining F.A.S.T. was a bit of a challenge for me. I was almost fearful of the process at times. I knew the process would be uncomfortable, but I also knew that life was going to continue to come at me F.A.S.T. and I needed to be ready. 2 Timothy 2:21 made me realize that I had to submit to the process of sanctification.

"Therefore, if anyone cleanses himself from what is dishonorable, he will be a vessel for honorable use, set apart as holy, useful to the master of the house, ready for every good work."

Although I didn't want to go through the growing pains that go along with the process of sanctification, I knew it was beyond necessary. I knew that this was the step that would free me from being run over by life. I knew I

I NEVER GOT

had to make a conscious effort to grow and become more anointed so the very thing that burdened me would no longer be my bondage.

Finally, all of this took time and time was on my side because God controls it. Oh, My Goodness...this was a time of great rejoicing for me. I no longer had to be fearful of life coming at me F.A.S.T. I know longer had to wonder if I'd be ready. I realized that I was making the correct preparation to be ready. I also realized that the continuum of events measured from the past to the future and right through my present were simply there to help me grow. Psalm 90:12 teaches us,

"So, teach us to number our days that we may get a heart of wisdom."

I realized that I had to learn the value of time and what it could yield for me. I couldn't just waste Gods time with all my stuff. I had to understand the outcome or net result of time from his point of view.

Wow! My entire view of life changed. Somewhere along my life's journey, the best advice I never got was right there anyway. It was right in front of me, but I couldn't see it. My parents didn't share this advice directly but in so many ways, they shared it indirectly. For that, and for them, I am grateful. Thankful.

THE BEST ADVICE

The best advice I never got was a glorious journey of personal development and growth that I would have missed had I not paid attention and fully submitted to the process. Oftentimes, we search for what we think we need when it is right in front of us the entire time. Don't be guilty of that. Advice is good but know that it can come in many ways. It can come in the form of a book you read or a lesson that you learn. It can come directly or indirectly. It can present itself formally or informally. What really matters is whether you catch it no matter how it comes.

The best advice I never got is **Life Comes at you F.A.S.T. – Be Ready,** but guess what, I got it any way!

You

are the Apple

of God's eye.

SHAWNEE PENKACIK is a wife to her husband Jason of twenty-two years. A mom to 11 amazing children – ages 4 years old to 21 years old. She is an author, a social media manager, and host a podcast. She has found throughout life that God is faithful and celebrates daily that the joy of the Lord is her strength. She loves to encourage and remind moms that they are enough in Christ. Her favorite thing is to spend time with her family or grab a cup of coffee in morning with her Bible. You can learn more about her at sunshinythoughts.com.

I DEDICATE

I would like to dedicate this chapter to my husband Jason and my children. Their love, encouragement, and support mean the world to me.

5. The Possibilities

When I look back at the experiences that I have had in life, I look at my childhood. I grew up in a small town with an average family. I grew up in a two-parent Christian home with just one younger brother. We had an average home with all that we needed. My father worked as a truck driver and my mother was a stay at home mom because back then it was important to focus on raising children.

I was taught family values of being polite, using your manners, and being respectful. The other thing I was taught was to grow up fast. I always had to be more than what I was. I was pushed beyond limits which in some aspect is a good thing. But in other ways, it caused me to miss out on my childhood. Growing up, I played with toys very little as it upset my mom if I had toys out. I had a toy kitchen that was my favorite and often dreamed of being a baker. This is very similar to my daughter now. She watches endless cake videos and dreams of making cupcakes for others.

I NEVER GOT

I was always asked what was ahead in my life. I was never taught to live in the moment or to enjoy the moments that had been given to me. My mother pushed me to do better, be more, and to sometimes go beyond my means. When I left home at age eighteen, I was very naïve and really did not know what life had to offer. I had been sheltered and left to experience life in a small box. I had a few friends who I trusted but I mostly was a bit of a loner.

I had the usual responsibilities that a child has of keeping their room tidy and other household chores. The only difference is that if I didn't do them, I got punished often harshly. The day that I left home, I had no idea what to expect. Home was my safety net. But I knew that it was time for me to step out of my comfort zone. Little by little challenges arose, I learned to face them but was often timid and scared. I relied on the encouragement of others around me to remind me that I could do hard things and be a success.

THE BEST ADVICE

On my first day at my new high school, I remember walking into those big halls and seeing people very different from me. Girls and guys with pink and blue hair, different kinds of clothing, and even piercings. These were things that we didn't see in my small town. These were things that defined city life. I was hesitant and wondering, "Could I fit in here?" "How will these people ever like a simple girl like me?" I attended my classes and often kept to myself. I was talked to as the new girl and since it was so late in the year, it was odd to the students as to why I would be starting over. Slowly I started to come out of my very tight turtle shell and instead of burying my head in the sand, I learned to make friends as these people didn't know my story. They liked me for who I was.

I graduated from high school after a lot of hard work, encouragement, and tears. When I came to Buffalo, I started dating a young man from our local church. My family immediately started to ask the questions that put pressure on our relationship, asking us "are you getting married? Are you going to college? What's next for your life?" Questions that are not necessarily bad questions but questions that make you feel pressured. After all, I was just eighteen years old. I had my whole life ahead of me and instead, everyone wanted me to yet again grow up.

I NEVER GOT

Growing up is difficult enough, but the pressure to be better and do more was still there. I knew that I had dreams that God had placed on my heart. From a young age, I knew the Lord was calling me to work in children's ministry. I had done it since I was a young girl. But I didn't know where. I had been drawn to my then boyfriend because of this. He worked in ministry as well. We seemed like a good fit. We understood each other, laughed together, and shared many memories that I would cherish. But my family would continue to ask for more. Growing up in the church, I was often told that the signs were everywhere, and that Jesus was returning. They made it sound like He was returning today or even tomorrow.

I knew that I wanted to live my life pleasing and acceptable to the Lord and I wanted to experience all that He had for me. "Well, you'll want to get married." My cousin would say. My other cousin was in the process of planning her second wedding. I just wanted to be me. But I didn't know what lay ahead for me. Instead of listening to the voice inside my heart, I listened to those around me. I wanted them to love me, I wanted to make them happy. I didn't want to be a disappointment anymore. And because of that, I rushed life. My boyfriend and I felt the pressures from my family and we just realized that we couldn't make our relationship work. He wanted to finish college and just enjoy the moment. I was pressuring him to commit because of succumbing to the peer pressure from my family and fear surrounding me. I heard the voices, "You have to experience life. There is only so much time left. Are you looking at the world events?"

I pushed the fast-forward button on life. I was introduced to my now husband of twenty-three years. I knew that we had chemistry. We spent a lot of time together, but we had different values, different views on things. My family and friends again pressured with the questions, "Where is this relationship going?" I had no clue. I started to talk about marriage and family, when I really should have just focused on being and learning. We got married at a very young age.

Not even two days into our marriage, a minister from my cousin's church told me that God was preparing me to be a mom. A mom? I was just nineteen years of age. I didn't know much about motherhood. I did know what I didn't want to do. I also knew of the good examples that I had of Godly mothers. Women who were my mentors, who had stepped in to teach me about God's love, how to really love your family, and how to be patient and not so harsh. But motherhood while it was a great idea, seemed like it needed more time. However, I wanted to be in God's will and took the word of the minister as gospel. I would find out later that he had information that I was already pregnant, which I was not, and that is why he chose to say what he had said at that moment.

THE BEST ADVICE

After a few months of actively trying and being asked by our family if we had been successful yet, we became pregnant. We were still trying to get to know each other. I didn't know all his quirks and he didn't know all of mine. Yes, we were in love and finding our way. But we had challenges as well. My advice instead would be taking your time and enjoy your new life together. Have those quiet dinners just the two of you, sit and talk about your hopes and dreams, talk about your future, take vacations together, and before you have children, really know each other. Don't be in such a rush just because everyone thinks that now that you got married, you need to have children. You just need to enjoy your life together. There will be time for children down the road.

We had a beautiful baby boy in March 1997. He was so perfect and such a joy. I still wanted to work and not be just a stay at home mom. But again, the fears and pressures set in. "A good mom stays at home with her children." "It's the husband's job to provide. You need to be home with your baby." "Babies who go to daycare grow up badly. You don't want your child to grow up to be a delinquent."

I NEVER GOT

I wanted the absolute best for my son, as most parents do. I decided to cut back on my work hours and do more of what everyone else wanted. I still worked, just not as much. I got to know my beautiful boy. We had many mornings watching television together and listening to him coo. Those are moments that I wouldn't trade. But not every mom is destined to stay at home. In some families, both parents must work to pay the bills. And just because a child goes to daycare does not mean that they will be a delinquent.

I'd like to say the pressures of my family and expectations would stop here but they did not. Shortly after our son was born, we were asked questions yet again. "Well don't you want a baby girl?" We had just had our son. "I always wanted a granddaughter." I should have answered back and said, "You have a grandson just enjoy him." But as my mother watched people around her having babies, she wanted to have a granddaughter of her own. I realize this was her dream and yes, I dreamed of having a daughter as well. I just needed to enjoy the blessings that God had given me.

THE BEST ADVICE

Yet again, I gave in to the pressure and we conceived another child. This child would be another boy. My family would yet again ask for another baby and another because they really wanted to have a granddaughter. I constantly felt like I was letting them down. I didn't know why God was not allowing us to have a baby girl. Maybe there was just something wrong with me. I thought I was a rotten daughter, so God won't give me a daughter because I wouldn't know how to raise her.

A few years later, after five beautiful boys, God gave us our daughter. She was born a few weeks early, needed time in NICU, but was otherwise perfect. She brought joy to everyone around her. I felt my family would be finally happy. They had all the boys and finally the granddaughter that they had desired. Then the questions from outsiders started. "Well, family planning is against God's will. If you use birth control, it will kill a baby. It's like abortion." I was against abortion, so I didn't want this. Yet again, listening to those voices and not my own. I made the decision to just trust the Lord with our family. Now, I don't regret this decision as I have eleven beautiful and amazing children. Our family is one of my greatest joys and is my greatest treasure. But the pattern continued of listening to outside voices and what others thought God's plan for my life needed to look like instead of me being strong enough to make those decisions based on what I knew God was speaking to me.

I finally decided to seek out a mentor which took a long time and start to ask her how I could really know if I was in God's will. I learned that I already was in God's will. I was doing what He wanted me to do. I was being the best wife and mom that I could be. I was helping those around me. I didn't need to be perfect for God. He loved me just the way I was. After all, in John 3:16, it says that "God so loved the world He gave his one and only son that whosoever believes in Him will not perish but will have everlasting life." That verse didn't say that God would love me if I was a stay at home mom and didn't have hopes and dreams. It didn't say God would love me if I had a daughter. It didn't say God would love me if I had the perfectly clean house that everyone felt I should have with six children under the age of eight.
However, the truth that I was missing in all these years was that I didn't need to measure up for God to love me. He already did. He loved me when I was single, married, had children, was just a mom of boys, and even now. He just loved me. I kept trying to earn the approval of my family and yes even of God. When I already had God's approval after all.

I started to slowly see myself as God saw me instead of how my family did. I saw myself as chosen, redeemed, loved, cherished, blessed, and so much more. My perspective started to change. I stopped trying to earn God's love and started to just walk in it. And life for me drastically changed. I became more confident, able to take steps of faith knowing that the Lord was taking me by the hand. Yes, family pressures were still there. I learned it was okay to have boundaries with family and set people at a distance. They didn't have to be in my inner circle. I learned to be a healthier, happier me. After all, God loved me for me. The Bible says that He would leave the ninety-nine just to look for the one. God cares about even just one soul.

The advice that I would give that I never received would be don't rush your life, trying to please those around you. You will always fall short. You will never meet their expectations as they will always change them. Instead look at God's opinion of you. See yourself as He sees you. Listen to His voice. Then you will truly have a blessed and fulfilled life.

You

are worth it.

THE BEST ADVICE

FRED "FUNKI" MILLS a Reidsville, NC native, is a vocalist, keyboardist, writer, arranger and producer with an extensive background in the music industry. He is the founder of the successful brand Sweet Dreams Productions and Band. Fred's mission is artist development and production in R&B, Smooth Jazz, and Neo Gospel. He has performed, produced, or recorded with artists such as Betty Davis (ex-wife of Miles Davis), Chops (horn section for The Police and Alicia Keys), Doug Wimbish (bassist for Living Colour), Cindy Mizelle (Luther Vandross and Steely Dan), Teddy Riley (Kids at Work), Atlantic Records, Sugarhill Records and Mercury Records.

6. Navigating Through Life

Born in a small southern town in 1950, I grew up in a vastly different social and cultural landscape compared to life today. However, "the more things change, the more they remain the same." I believe every generation usually wants the same thing; a fruitful life.

As you navigate through life's journey there will be turns; U-turns, one-way and do not enter signs, and many other warnings and directions. Just when you think your route is perfect, you find that life's GPS is constantly updating. You will discover the landscape of life is continuously changing.

The one thing that you can rely upon in life is that we have choices. Your decision making will determine your destiny. Many of us make decisions one of two ways; on our own or based on the advice from others. I have made a lot of choices in my life and have also been the recipient of too much advice. I was advised to go to college. I chose to join the army and become a paratrooper. I was still in my teens; impulsive and didn't really have a clue about life. I did attend college after the army.

In your early years it seems like you must listen to anyone's advice that is older than you.

This is especially true if you look up to them or they appear to know things you don't. As I became older, I realized that we often confuse opinions with advice. You can figure that out later.

What's most important is having a destination in your life, and a planned route. Be sure to plan for delays, detours, unexpected events and rest stops. Planning and preparation are key.

Make life as enjoyable as possible and remember it's not a spectator sport. You will have to be engaged. Family, relationships, education, community, religion and politics are all going to play a big part in navigating through life. The amount of control you have on your life will depend upon the investment you make in becoming an independent thinker. I say "the amount" of control because there are things that will affect your life where you will have little or no control. There will always be some situations that require an adjustment in your attitude.

Because you can't control a situation doesn't mean you are wrong in your beliefs. Racism, prejudice, sexism, equal justice and political correctness are just a few things that may test your
beliefs. As much as we want to be individuals, we must coexist if we desire to make contributions to society. Life is also a team sport.

Life is a live and learning experience. Each day you have an opportunity to gain knowledge and understanding. Always be open to new ideas, concepts, and technology. Be a leader when you can and a follower if the situation is worthy. Never sell out! Always, always be true to yourself!

Be conscious of how you embrace the concept of love. It will play a very important role in life.
Relationships will come and go, but if you are blessed you will find that true love. Sex can

sometimes create an illusion of love, masked in lust. It's in your best interest to make the distinction. When you remove sex from the equation, it is possible to experience something like the love you feel for parents, siblings and others of a non-sexual relationship.

Be patient and never lower your standards. Being in a relationship can bring the greatest and most precious gift from God, children. Becoming a parent will change everything. You will understand love in a brand-new way. Priorities and responsibilities change with parenthood. Unlike many other relationships, this is a Lifetime commitment. Be prepared for a great experience.

We all strive to be happy in life. You will learn that happiness comes and goes. A great home life, a job that you love, financial security, and good friends play an important role in your happiness. There will however be times when other factors invade your happy place with sadness, anger, disgust and fear. The world can sometimes be a very dark place if you care about your fellow man. Whatever the circumstance, always try to find some happiness and joy in troubled times.

I have been extremely fortunate in having strong women in my life. Raised by a loving single mother, grandmother, and aunts. It was a time when neighbors, teachers, and even the church community had a vested interest in making sure children were educated, nurtured, and disciplined. Later in life I would be blessed with an incredibly strong woman to become my wife. Marriage can be a wonderful thing when you put the work in. I learned a lot from my three sisters, two older and one younger: a pastor, an educator/administrator, and a Dean of a Law School. They set examples and taught me the who, what, why and when of growing up even after I thought I was a man. It truly takes a village to raise a child.

Because I have faced a few challenges recently, I want to share something I believe to be essential to life, Good Health. Nothing matters as much as good physical, mental and spiritual health. Being in sync with one's overall health allows you the freedom to accomplish the challenges presented daily. Take care of your body and mind by eating right, exercising, getting enough sleep and continuing to expand your intellect. Whatever your religious preference, be involved in spiritual growth.

THE BEST ADVICE

Respect, honesty, trustworthiness, and humility are a few of the valuable characteristics on should possess. I have so much more I would like to share. I hope what I have given will be helpful. In the end, "Life is what you make it." Be bold, be committed, and be righteous in everything you do.

Finally, keep family close but keep God closer. In your search for answers, remember that –
"Knowledge is not free; you have to pay attention."
Peace......

Nothing can stop

You – except You.

CELETHA RILEY has dedicated her life to her family, ministry, and community. Her varied experiences have equipped her to be a stellar wife, mom, mentor, and community leader. Her marriage has led her to create the "I Choose You Marriage Ministry". This ministry is built on the key principles of God, prayer, respect, communication, bonding, unity, and submission. Celetha and her husband of 9 years, David D. Riley co-host conference calls twice a month. They also oversee a private virtual community and are the founders of The Temple of Faith Ministry, Spiritual growth and Personal development are areas that she fosters in. Many have been impacted by her legacy of ministering The Gospel, through women's, prison, and, outreach to hurricane and disaster ministries.

I DEDICATE

I would like to dedicate this to my husband, Prophet David Riley, and my three children; D'Andr'e, Diaundrea, and Alicia, for all your support and love.

7. Soul Tie FREE

The best advice that I never got was about soul-ties. Had I known what I know today, I would have waited until I became married to have intercourse, and children. Growing up in the ghetto, from a large family, I witnessed many unwed teenage mothers, and girls with multiple children, from multiple partners. I never heard much conversation about weddings, keeping your virginity, or waiting until after you finished school to have intercourse. There was a lot of peer pressure to start getting involved in sexual activity at an early age. Basically, engaging into intercourse while young, was perceived as the norm. Therefore, seeing and hearing what was taking place with many young girls involved in sexual activity wasn't shocking to me at all.

I had goals to finish school, go to the military, and then obtain my nursing degree. The overall goal was to have a great life for myself. I started dating around the tender age of 13, up until I became pregnant in the 11th grade. Due to my pregnancy, I had to enroll into Cope North Alternative School for young pregnant teenage mothers. While attending this school, I realized that I was surrounded by young, single teenage mothers, who were also never taught about abstinence or waiting until marriage. In fact, many of them bragged about having multiple partners. It was then when I realized how lost we all were, in an environment growing up fast with no true role models. We lacked role models to show us how to practice abstinence, and establish a healthy relationship with a partner, which could then lead to marriage and children.

Even though I made that realization mentioned prior, during the following year, in the 12th grade, I became pregnant again. I managed to give birth six months before my high school graduation. All the previous dreams I had of going to the military and obtaining my nursing degree, were no longer. I was truly devastated and wondering how I, a single teenage mother with two kids, would survive and make a great future for myself and my children. With two kids, and there fathers not present, I promised myself that I wouldn't leave my two children behind.

While trying to figure out life for myself and my children, I met a young man. This would be the man that I had my last child with and shared the next ten years of my life with. During this relationship, I was emotionally and mentally abused. During the ten years, I'd try to leave the relationship on several occasions, but would always end up back in his arms. I knew I wanted better for myself and my children, but I would always end up in the same predicament repeatedly. It was then that I constantly asked myself, "What keeps drawing me back to this unhealthy, toxic abusive environment?" The behavior didn't change, the words got worse, yet I kept accepting apology after apology. I wasn't happy, yet, I didn't know what to do.

I NEVER GOT

One day, as I was having a conversation with a colleague from work, she shared her experience with me. Like myself, she had undergone abuse in a relationship. She said that once she started talking to God, and listening to the teachings from her Pastor, it was then she realized why she kept repeating the same patterns. As we continued speaking, she shared with me that I was soul tied. That is the reason why I kept returning to him and having constant thoughts about him or my other former partners. Not quite understanding what my colleague meant, I asked that she break the term "soul ties" down for me. Soul ties occur when one has sexual intercourse with an individual/s, and your womb/soul is still attached to whom you had sexual intercourse with. The issue arises when one never receives deliverance to break the attachments from that individual. Therefore, it's easier to continue interacting with a toxic individual, who you aren't spiritually free from.

THE BEST ADVICE

As the years passed, I continued to study more and learned how to break free from that toxic relationship, or so I thought. Now married to my first husband, I realized that I wasn't completely free. I brought a lot of experiences from my previous relationship, into my marriage. Anger, stubbornness, and mean-spiritedness were attributes that I now noticed of myself. Those attributes, along with other issues, led to my divorce. After my divorce, I broke down. Still that young girl deep inside, yearning for a stable healthy relationship that I never witnessed, I just wanted to be happy. I poured my heart and soul out, and asked God to help me. I truly just wanted every soul tie from past relationships broken, and to stop hindering me from pursuing a healthy relationship.

It was then that I was completely honest with myself. To fix the problem, I had to acknowledge the root of it. I had soul ties from the sexual encounters with my children's fathers, and now my ex-husband. Soul ties can cloud your judgement and actions. This cloudiness consisted of pushing away those that are truly trying to love you, and feeling, as well as thinking unhealthy thoughts about yourself. I begin to pray to God and wish that someone would've told me that it was okay to be a virgin and save yourself for marriage.

If not discovered and broken early on, unclean spirits and behaviors can be picked up from partners and can last a lifetime. You may be saying to yourself that you have never really thought about it like this. But yes, soul ties are the reason why you constantly fantasize about your ex or can't move on after being in a relationship. You will act like them, display habits like theirs, then ask yourself "why am I acting this way?", when you've been ended the relationship with them. You can't seem to get over them, because soul ties affect your thoughts, actions, and decisions.

Soul ties affect the following five core areas: will, memory, intellect, emotions, and imagination. Each area is important and is interdependent on the other. If not strong in one area, then it will adversely affect the other. The following briefly describes each area and explains how soul ties adversely affects each;

- *Will: one's will describe the desire for change to occur, or to allow for oneself to become open for change.*

- *Memory: with memory being the facility that stores past events, one's memory can constantly play ill events and thoughts. The memory can place false illusions to make one think that the situation isn't as bad as it seems.*

- *Intellect: intellect coincides with the inability to think highly of oneself, therefore, affecting the self-esteem. Constant thoughts or habits that may inhibit the intellect can be comparing yourself to others, always doubting yourself, and not being able to accomplish anything.*

- *Emotions: some habits that coincide with your emotions and soul ties, are: constant crying for no apparent reason, feeling unstable, feeling depressed, or expressing sudden surges of anger.*

- *Imagination: imagination involves the formation of new ideas, and concepts. Soul ties affect the imagination by forming unhealthy thoughts. These thoughts consist of being unable to visualize yourself in the future, and constantly drawing you to past environments.*

The goal to being free is to address each of the five areas. You must have to will to live, overcome, and break all unhealthy soul ties. Focus your memory on positive areas such as when you were strong, happy, and achieving great accomplishes in life. You must continue to tell yourself as often as necessary that, *"I am a strong intellectual being. I make healthy and positive decisions. My mindset is focused, and I am eager to live a healthier life. I have taken control of my emotions, and I am not unstable. I can think clearly without allowing my emotions to dictate which decision I should make. I will have a better outcome than previously. My imagination now includes me seeing myself healthy and being content with my decisions that will be made."* Everything mentioned was achieved once I learned how to break all those soul ties. I can only imagine how my life would have been had I known as a teenager, the importance of waiting until marriage. Therefore, I wouldn't had opened my soul up to any sexual unhealthy soul ties.

But don't worry, because you don't need to go through this alone. If you feel as though you are dealing with soul ties, I assure you that there is help readily available. To fix the issue, you must immediately recognize the problem in its early stages. Once recognized, partner up with a dedicated sister prayer warrior, that you can share your experience with. It's important to have a healthy life and maintain healthy relationships because that is what God desires for us. The more you become familiar with recognizing soul ties, the more you can help the next sister get freed from them.

I NEVER GOT

It is my prayer that the advice that I have shared is beneficial to many young ladies all over the world. This is the best advice I and so many others never got. **I love the idea of family, values, and stability.** We must educate our young girls as early as possible, so that they can look forward to marriage. Marriage can create a solidified foundation, resulting in less single parent homes, and a decrease of issues such as criminal activity, and school dropout rates among adolescents. Therefore, this teaching can assist young females in realizing how valuable they are, then they can share this information among their peers, or someone they may be dating.

Even though the topic of soul ties has been discussed in relevance to dating, and sexual intercourse, it is also important that young females strive to have healthy relationships in general - establishing healthy relationships with family relatives and peers are critical. *It is important that young females choose their friends wisely.* If a peer or family member displays negative habits, it is possible that you can attach yourself to that behavior as well. Make a conscious decision to say no, I will not repeat the same pattern, or behaviors as them. I want to live a healthier life, make the right choices, and become a productive citizen. For me to achieve, I cannot allow this soul tie or generational curse to attach itself to me. I will break the cycle, be more attentive, discover who I am, my potential, and pursue it with everything within me. It's attainable because of this valuable information that has been given to me, helping me to realize why many individuals make bad choices, and often go off course.

I am grateful to have been given this opportunity to share this information with you.

You are

free!

THE BEST ADVICE

CHOU HALLEGRA is a Certified Counselor and Life Coach, and a Transformational Speaker. She is on a mission to help people rise above their circumstances. She is passionate about empowering people to achieve emotional wellness, reach their full potential and live fulfilling lives. Through her many life challenges, Chou has learned to turn her stumbling blocks into stepping stones and she now teaches others how to do the same. Chou and her family reside in South Central PA. You reach her at www.graceandhopeconsulting.com .

I DEDICATE

I dedicate this writing piece to all the girls who are seeking for love. You are already loved. Accept that love and rest in it.

8. YOU ARE LOVED

I wish I knew sooner rather than later that I was loved. I'm sure my parents loved me somehow. They provided a safe place for me to live, made sure I ate, and got me clothes. I had what I needed and I'm sure everyone would agree that I was well taken care of. However, in my young brain, I didn't equate that with being loved. Not knowing that I was loved affected me in so many ways. Perhaps the damage could have been avoided. Nevertheless, I'm glad I took hold of the truth that changed my life for the better.

The Confusion

My parents separated when I was five years old. I lived in Brazzaville, Congo (Africa) at the time. I was told that my mom received a letter from my father while he was still in Europe asking her to vacate the premises. I don't remember all the details, but I recall that once my father returned from his medical training in Europe, he slept in my uncle's rom and I was in my mom's room. I don't remember them talking at all. I was later told that my mom was given three days to leave.

That day finally came, whether it was three days or longer, I don't know. But that day, my mom's belongings were all loaded in a taxi. I clung to her as she was my primary caregiver for those short five years. I screamed, "I want to go with mommy", so with her I went. I wasn't sure what to expect. I was only five. What did the future hold? What happened to my family? I didn't know, and nobody provided any explanation. After staying with my mom for a few days, I somehow returned to my dad. I'm not sure how that came to be, except the fact that my dad was a medical doctor and had more financial security to provide for me.

After returning to my father's house, I was then raised by a new mom. My stepmother arrived from America and raised me as her own. I don't have any memory of seeing my mom for the next five years. I don't know what the reasons were; again, nobody explained anything. It wasn't until a civil war erupted in my country that I got to see my mom again; that's the first memory I have of her since the time I returned to live with my dad. I grew up in a culture where people expected children to just go with the flow, without explaining anything to them. Unfortunately, this causes lot of emotional damages that can linger for years.

A couple years after that civil war, my dad and I relocated to the United States to join my stepmother. She had left the country during the civil war. Since she and my sister were the only American citizens in our family at that time, the US embassy evacuated them out of the war zone.

I arrived in US at the age of eleven years old and a year later I was sent back to Africa. My father had to go work overseas with an international organization and my stepmom was raising me and my 2 younger siblings. I'm sure it was hard, and she needed help, so I returned to Brazzaville where I stayed for eight years.

Once I was back in Africa, I lived with my biological mother. It took some time to get to know each other. She probably remembered me as a five-year-old and I had no idea how to relate to her. We clashed. She was mad at me for things I didn't think was my fault. And I did things that she didn't understand. We had cultural differences to overcome. Afterall, I raised by an American mother and now I had to fit into the Congolese culture. We had different personalities and temperaments. We had to work on our relationship.

I NEVER GOT

During my time back in Congo, I received a few letters from my stepmom but didn't hear much from my dad. I later learned that my stepmom sent more things than what I received, including packages. Unfortunately, the postal service in Congo, just isn't the best so not all my mail and packages were delivered. It appeared that my father didn't write to me during that time. I heard from him about six years later when we started the immigration progress for me to return to the US.

Like with many things in my childhood, I didn't receive any details about what had happened to me. Why weren't my parents together anymore? Why couldn't I stay with my mom when she first left? How come my mom never contacted me during those five years prior to the civil war? Why did I have to be sent back to Congo? Why didn't my dad contact me way before we started the immigration process again? Didn't he notice that six years have passed by?

I lived for years as if those things didn't bother me but as I got older, I realized that the things that happened to me in my childhood created lot of confusion about what love is. Can people love and be so distant? Can people love and act as if their actions don't affect others? These questions were never answered, and my confusion grew bigger.

The Void

My childhood experiences shaped how I related to people, how I perceived life, and how I saw myself. I grew up very conservative, and I thank God for that. However, inside of me I longed for the father I never had and the mother I wished I had. And that longing led me to cling to people longer than I should, just because I had a need, the need to be loved.

I had my first boyfriend at the age of fifteen. All seemed well, until I was pressured to do things, I didn't feel comfortable doing. I was told, "you'll do it if you loved me". Did I love this person? Did I even know what love was? I gave in and then everything changed. I went to spend Summer at my grandpa's, in a different town, and when I returned, I was told that my boyfriend was seeing other girls. I wasn't sure how to take it. He made up some stories of being alone and in my confusion, I believed him. I forgave and clung to him, and the same thing happened repeatedly.

We were together on and off for a couple years. He would walk away with another girl and then would return and say he loved me. In my confusion, I would get back with him. The cycle went on and on with no change. While this was going on, I came to faith in Christ and eventually broke off with that boyfriend. But a void still existed in my heart.

I NEVER GOT

I got married a few years later, at the age of twenty-one. I had committed my life to Christ and married someone I had known to be a mature Christian. The first five years of our marriage was a long-distance relationship due to immigration issues, but I went overseas five times to visit him. During those years, there were many incidents where I questioned his commitment to me and to the family that we started together. I felt as if the kids and I were not a priority for him. Once he came to the US, those feelings were confirmed time and time again.

I had hoped that we could have worked things out; but while I was chasing after him, he was chasing after others. We separated three years after he arrived in this country and three years after that we were divorced. That was a full decade of me striving for his love. He must have loved me at some point, because he pursued me first. When he asked me out, I prayed about it and then said, "Yes". It was a successful marriage, but I don't regret the children we had together, my kids are everything to me.

It wasn't until the separation that I started to do some serious soul-searching and began to truly work on myself. During that intense time of self-discovery and healing, I realized that I been trying to fill a void for all those years. Although I didn't have many romantic relationships, the few that I had provided the acceptance and reassurance I didn't receive from my dad, and the comfort I didn't receive from my mom. I had the need to feel loved so when people said or showed me that they loved me, I clang to them. I would run after them even when they clearly showed me that I wasn't a priority for them. This caused more emotional damage instead of filling the void I had since I was a child.

I had the need to be reassured that I was loved no matter what. I needed to hear "I love you". I needed to be told, "I'm proud of you". My father valued education and as I was growing up, I made it a priority to always be at the top of my class, or at least among the top three. I didn't realize that was my way of trying to gain the attention of my father, although he wasn't always there to notice, nor did he ask about it.

When I was married, I tried to do everything to please my husband. It wasn't necessarily because I wanted to or because I felt it was the best thing to do. I did many things because deep inside I needed his approval. I needed his acceptance. I craved those things because I didn't get them in my childhood, when I needed them the most, when I was still forming my view of self and of the world. I needed a major shift, otherwise I would be stuck in people-seeking and people-pleasing forever.

The Change

As I worked on myself during that difficult season after my separation with my now ex-husband, something inside of me shifted and that changed everything. The more I spent time with God, the more my eyes and heart were opened to His love for me.

I came to the realization that nobody on earth would ever love me perfectly. Not my father, not my mother, not even my husband. All their love, even if given in their highest capabilities will always come short because they are broken humans just like I am. That was a tough pill to swallow but one that unlocked my breakthrough.

THE BEST ADVICE

As a child I needed and wanted my parents' love, and rightfully so. Every child should know and feel that they're loved. That foundation is so important for their development. Without it, they confuse what love is and might seek for love in all the wrong ways and in all the wrong places. Even when love is given in a healthy way, it's important to realize that people are humans and as humans they can fail us. They will make mistakes and they might hurt us even when they don't intend to. As I grew intellectually, mentally, emotionally, and spiritually, I understood that my parents and even my ex-husband had (and have) their own emotional wounds that they need to process and heal from.

My parents grew up in a culture where things were not discussed with children. Children's input was not sought, and their understanding was not a priority. Unfortunately, that leaves children feeling unimportant and invisible. My parents were also raised in a culture where love was not expressed openly. They weren't told that they were loved so they didn't tell me that they loved me, although in their hearts they did love me. And It wasn't until I came back to the US in my teen years that I personally learned to express love verbally.

My relationship with my parents has since changed tremendously. Both my parents are involved in my life. I keep in touch with my mom who is still in Africa. She encourages me and prays for me. My father is here in the US and he's more active in my life now, more than he ever did. Recently, he helped me move, installed new mirrors in my van, and paid for my children's extra-curricular activities. The more I realized that my parents were also in need of love, the less needy I felt. The less I expected from them, the more love I received.

It became easier for me to see and receive love from others once I grasped how much I was already loved. Because human love is fallible, we can't depend on it. It's nice to be loved by others but we can't live for people's approval, that creates an emotional prison for ourselves and leads to behaviors and relationships that are unhealthy.

We were already loved even before we were born. God knew each one of us way before we were formed in our mothers' wombs. That process alone proves that we were meant to be here. The original cell from which we came to be was one in million. You were handpicked to be here because God loved you that much. This is the truth that changed everything for me.

It didn't matter if others loved me "the right way" because I was already loved in the perfect way. Furthermore, this perfect love led Jesus to die on the cross, just for me, just for you. Even when we didn't know Him, He still loved us that much. And that, is love worth holding onto. God's love is the only love that will never fail us, the only love that is truly unconditional. You don't have to earn it, you don't have to prove that you deserve it. All you need to do is accept it. It's the gift of God's perfect love.

Knowing that God loved me that much made me cling to Him even more. I no longer strive for human love but for His love only. The more I seek Him, the more He fills me with His love so that I can share that love with others. Additionally, He puts the lonely into families. He has done it for me, providing many people who love me and treat me like family, especially when I felt like I had none. If you're struggling to feel loved, I invite you to take Him up on this offer. You are already loved because God loves you no matter what.

Here are some Bible verses that would help you better understand this perfect love: 1 John 3:1, Jeremiah 31:3, John 3:16, John 15:13, and Romans 5:8.

Don't look for love in all the wrong places, perfect love is available to you!

You are

blessed.

ALMENA L. MAYES is a woman who loves helping people reach their divine potential. As a mother, minister, mentor, teacher and best-selling author, she has been able to positively touch the lives of many young women. She strives to give context to the plight of women today and show them that no matter where they have been what counts is where they are going!

I DEDICATE

To my daughters Allorren and Dia, and Tameika who inspire me daily.

To my sons Darius and Mike who cover me completely.

And to my grandchildren Aurianna, Yendi, Catherine, Grayson and Michael who motivate me to be better every day.

9. My Daughters – and My Son!

I'm sure we all have moments in life that we would change if given the opportunity. Life comes at us fast and those spur of the moment or heat of the moment decisions can become pivotal. They can shape the life you have into one you have always dreamed of or one you have had nightmares about. I was the type of person who always worried about every choice I've ever made. I lived my life in the "what ifs". What if they don't like me? What if I fail? What if he is the wrong guy? What if I don't sleep with him...what if he leaves me...what if...

The advice I wish I had gotten is composed of three parts.

First, yesterday is over. There is nothing you can do to improve it. The choices and decisions made yesterday are done. If you made a mistake, learn from it and do better. Regret is an enemy to personal peace. In addition, it serves no purpose other than to keep you stuck in the past.

I NEVER GOT

Yes, there are some mistakes that have permanent affects. If a person finds himself incarcerated for an extended period, then his live may be forever altered. People who have been through traumatic experiences as a result of poor choices might find themselves in life changing predicaments. Words may be spoken that can never be taken back thus leaving relationships or friendships irreparable. However tragic it may feel these situations are, the fact is they happened. They are over. You didn't die. Life goes on.

We can reflect on what yesterday meant to our overall lives, accept that what is done is done, learn from it and move on. We cannot allow ourselves to get caught up in that reflection day after day. If we do, we end up in this perpetual loop of self-loathing, self-doubt and regret. We end up feeling sorry for ourselves and immobilized by the fear of making another misstep.

It takes a level of maturity, patience, faith and a positive attitude to give yourself a second chance to be successful. You can't allow your fear of failing again to hinder your future. As you go from day to day, what you believe to be true will always be your reality. If you rest in your past failures, you will see failure around every corner and beyond every door. Fear left unchecked becomes hopelessness. Hopelessness leads to inaction.

THE BEST ADVICE

What should you do to get beyond fear of yesterday? You must renew your thoughts! Make a definitive choice to change bad habits, end vitriolic relationships and get over yourself! Create a new mindset by renewing your mind! Live, learn and dedicate your time to changing the things that lead to your past failures. It won't happen overnight but if you stick to it, change will happen. Don't let fear of yesterday's mistakes frame your future.

Second, live, laugh and love today. I find that I smile almost all the time. I do my best to live my life fully every day. I am not saying that bad things don't happen to me; I have MS and a bad heart, I'm just saying I refuse to let the bad things shape the way I look at life.

How we chose to live life determines the life we live! I have learned to concentrate on the things that matter the most. I do my best to bring positivity into any space I occupy. I make a conscious choice to smile at someone I don't know, tell someone how beautiful he or she is and compliment someone else's positivity. I intentionally ask someone, "How are you?" and I genuinely listen to the answer. Being kind to people brings kindness back into your own life.

I challenge myself every day to be better than I was the previous day. I look for opportunities to learn something new, to face a difficult task or to have a new adventure.

I NEVER GOT

If there is something that seems ridged and predictable in my life, I choose to do something else. I have learned not to be afraid to shake things up. I have gone bungee jumping, dirt track racing and parasailing. I plan to go skydiving if I can ever meet the weight requirement. However, if I never get to jump from a plane, I will have had a wonderful affair with delicious!

I savor the little enjoyable moments. When I see one of my students grasp a difficult concept or I help an author push through writer's block; when I conquer a personal challenge or make someone laugh out loud, I find myself lying in bed, smiling uncontrollably.

Every day I do something that I enjoy doing. Some days I write, other days I sing karaoke. I might go get my nails and feet done or a massage. I ride my bike or hang out with my friends listening to live music. It just depends on what feels good in the moment. That's the key! Live in the moment! I wish someone had told me that moments are fleeting and once they are gone you can't get them back. I had to learn to value the time I have. I make every moment count. I once read somewhere, "Everybody dies but only a few live." I decided that I would live every today like it was going to be my last today! I would never again worry about yesterday or fear tomorrow.

Finally, I give myself permission to let tomorrow happen naturally. I don't borrow any stress or fear from it. I don't worry about whether it is even coming. I live in my "now". I only focus on what is going on around me right now! I'm not saying that I don't plan. I'm just saying that planning for the future is not so important that I miss out on the present. I don't think about what happens when the roses die, I just enjoy the fragrance the exude today.

It took a while, but I learned to accept things as they are. Worrying about what may or may not happen can cause undue stress. I am 53 years old and I don't need any extra wrinkles caused by anticipatory worrying. I live in a place of, "what's the worst that could happen?" Once I come to terms with that, I find that I have no reason to worry. Try it…it really works to quell the "what ifs". What if I lose my job? I'll get another one or I will work for myself. I may have to downsize a few things, but it won't kill me! If it doesn't kill me, I can do better. Some things that seem horrible are not so bad when you turn them over and really look at them.

I wish someone had told me that life constantly changes. Once I realized that and learned to go with the flow, I found myself much happier. I learned to stop clinging to places, things and people. All of them can be lost in an instant but what you have inside, your true self, is what will remain. Besides, clearing out the clutter always sets us up for growth.

I wish someone had told me to become excited by the prospect surprises. Live for the excitement and thrill of discovering a new day and a new opportunity to be your best self.

I've learned to live for the wisdom of yesterday, the smiles of today and the promise of tomorrow. That is the lesson I share with my daughters – and my son!

You are a Genius.

 **TOSHA DEARBONE** was born in Urania, Louisiana and raised in Houston, Texas. She is a mother of four, grandmother of one, Community Advocate, Founder of Positive Express, Certified Medical Assistant, Certified Nursing Assistant, Certified Community Health worker, Mentor, and an Author. Tosha specializes in medical care, educating young ladies and women about HIV and AIDS, domestic/sexually violence, self-esteem, and the voice for breaking generational curses. Tosha found her passion for young ladies through her own testimony of youth experiences and building a relationship with God. Tosha can be reached on social media at:

Tosha R Dearbone and via email trdearbo@yahoo.com.

I DEDICATE

I dedicated this to all young ladies that feel like they just cannot move forward after a mistake. Rise and keep going Queen!

10. Never Give Up!

Thinking back to the time, I was learning how to tie my shoes and how overwhelmed I was. I could hear the impatience in my mother voice; *"You will never get it if you continue to whine and not try".* Feeling so disappointed and afraid that I would never get it, I begin to try making little bunny ears. Hitting the YouTube button repeatedly. Replaying the song, *"Bunny ears, Bunny ears, playing by a tree. Criss-crossed the tree, trying to catch me. Bunny ears, Bunny ears, jumped into the hole, popped out the other side beautiful and bold."*

Then one day I was sitting on the bedroom floor practicing and out of nowhere I started screaming "Momma, Momma I got it!! I got it! I was so excited that I begin crying. My mom come walking in the room trying to make out what I said, and she said, "I knew you could do it if you continued to try". All I could do was smile. That was an exciting day for me! Looking back over the excitement of that day makes me think about how I could have used that same advice "…. whining and not trying" – later in my life.

THE BEST ADVICE

In 1995 my mother took me to the clinic to get an abortion. I was so scared. They begin setting up the sterile tools on a metal table and then had me to get undressed. Shortly after they said we are done, and I got up to get dressed.

On the way home, I felt confused and somewhat hurt because I heard about abortions but never thought I would be in that situation. Our ride home was silent and when we arrived at our house, everything just went back to normal, as if nothing had happened.

The following year came around 1996 and me and my younger brother would go to Louisiana every summer to stay with family. One night I became very sick. I could not keep no food down and I was feeling weak. So, my mother's friend called my mom and my mom suggested that she would come get us early. Ready to go home but not thinking about why I was sick. We arrived back in Houston and Monday morning was finally here. My mom took me to the clinic to see what was wrong. As we were awaiting the doctor to return to the room we sat patiently. The doctor enters the room and just the thought of what if instantly played in my head and the thoughts of my heart stopped, not really but I was so shocked to hear the doctor read back my results "Your pregnant test is positive". I instantly became sick and afraid to hear what my mother had to say. On the ride

I NEVER GOT

home, it was silent - again. We pulled up to the house and I get out to go inside the house. While entering my room I could feel my mother walking behind me and she says, "So what you going to do"? I pause for a moment, "I am going to keep it." She abruptly left the room. I was so confused and worried about what to honestly do.

When my boyfriend and tell him the news but all he did was sit quietly on the phone. You could hear him breathing. I ask him what he thought we should do? He a child himself, so he didn't know what to do any more than I did. Leaving me to make the final decision. In that moment all I could think of was having someone in the world to truly love me. But I also know that having a baby would not keep my boyfriend around.

In just 9 short months, I had become a teenage, single mother. I loved my child, but I was frustrated with my circumstances – a teen mom!

I had a desire to finish high school, I didn't think that having a child should stop me from having goals and dreams. So, I enrolled in a program that I believed would allow me to complete my high school education, only to find out that the program would only permit me to earn a GED and I did not want *just* a GED. Another disappointment! Then I meet this guy – and he was very nice to me. Spent time with me, bought me things – it

THE BEST ADVICE

all seemed so good. But he was an abuser! He left me hurt and alone.

But I never gave up on God, or should I say He never gave up on me. I felt so unworthy, because I had allowed my relationship with God to fall by the waste-side. I constantly beat myself up with negative words, and to make matters worse, my two brothers above me would say negative things to me and about me.

By then, I not only was I dealing with feeling abandoned, rejected, alone, unloved, etc., I simply wanted to give up. I would look at my children and try to encourage myself. I wanted to believe that I could make it, that I could turn things around. Thank God that He never left me!

The truth was that I was alone. I had no real guidance. I was a young girl trying to figure it all out. But God was there with me every step of the way – leading me and guiding me, even when I didn't realize He was.

Daughter remember that you are never alone.

Soon, I decided to try the dating game again. Only this time, I had two children to consider. I wasn't if I was completely ready, but I wanted to be loved and cared for – and the best way I know to get that, was to give it to someone – hoping they would return my kindness.

I NEVER GOT

One I met a guy at a night club, and we begin dating. Just having fun and hanging out. Then things started to get a little more serious yet dangerous because he was the type of person that love to have a bunch of female friends. Whom he always called sisters. Until one day I realized this sister was no sister and I instantly wanted to break things off but couldn't. Not only did I want out but here I am pregnant with baby number three. *"What have I done?"* I hung my head and asked God, "Why me? Why do I continue to go in the cycle of bad relationships, abuse, feeling down on myself, and thinking that I just cannot be alone?" God is silent. And there I was single again with not two babies but three.

"God does it get any easier? Will I ever come out of this pattern?" "Breathe", He said. **"You are not your mistakes."**

While pregnant I enrolled in school to become a Medical Assistant. On the last day of class I went into labor. I begin shouting and praising God it did not set off my expected graduation date in October 2004. I made it. I begin to feel so good about myself because I had completed something that I wanted to do.

Two months had gone by and I was offered a position at a behavioral facility where I begin to get my training skills and foot in the door of what the medical field truly

THE BEST ADVICE

look like. While working I tried to stay to myself and not mingle too much, but this one person caught my attention. Yes, it was a guy. My flesh begins to become weak again. Feeling as though I needed someone. He would flirt with me, make jokes, and from time to time I would take him home after work. Then one day he asked me "Are you seeing anyone"? I said no. He leaned in and kiss me and from there we begin dating.

Things were moving fast. Before I knew it, we were moving in to together, I was getting a new job, and a new car. Everything was going great! A little to great as some would say. A little over a couple of months had passed by and I begin to feel nauseous. I could not eat, sleep, nor stay focused. But for whatever reason I did not even second guess myself, I knew I was pregnant. I went to the store bought a home pregnant test and it tested positive. Instantly I begin to ask myself why? Why have I allowed myself to fall in this position again? Don't I love myself enough not to keep allowing this to happen? Days went by and now it's time to go to the doctor and they confirmed it. Baby number four was on the way but the only thing different was he was not trying to leave me, cheat on me, beat on me, etc. I started to believe I found someone who loved me.

As time went by a scripture kept being revealed to me;

I NEVER GOT

Matthew 7:6 KJV, "Give not that which is holy unto the dogs, neither cast ye your pearls before swine, lest they trample them under their feet, and turn again and rend you."

So, I kept asking God why was this scripture continued to pop up? Little did I know the truth it was about to be reveal. Child father number four was no different than the other three. He was a cheater, a promiscuous liar, and an individual that hit on women also. Yes, the domestic violence was back again. Now it was starting to look like a trend and I all I could think of if I had someone to tell me right from wrong, give me advice, guide me, show me what true love was, and help me identify myself for me. I just may could have avoided some of this heartache and despair. I would see my parents fighting, arguing and my brothers hit on women as if it was okay. So, I felt I was no diffcrent.

Days went by and I knew I had to make a move, so I packed up and moved to my mom house. I want to say me, and my children lived there for about six months and then we found a townhouse. I was trying to get back on track. Financial income was not the best, but it was enough to start over and get back on my feet. I begin to change my perspective and tell myself for this to work I must start declaring it. Every day I would get up and look in the mirror and speak over myself. In order to change I must believe it. So, time begin to go by, and I had come to self and begin to speak the changes that needed to occur for this pattern to end. I started to accept that I was fine with being by myself if I was busy, but if I slowed down it was like the devil was trying to attack me. I would get in my flesh. Thinking I wanted a man but for whatever reason I just could not get the attention of anyone. At least not the ones I believed were my type.

In year 2013 I begin dating my old childhood boyfriend and we became engaged early 2014. So much was going on that the kids were enjoying themselves, we were getting along, and I was just thankful. I was beginning to think I found the one. Until one night we begin to get phone calls, phone calls that lead me and him to begin arguing. He was cheating. I felt like my world was just turned upside down again. I could not catch a break. He tried hard to make it right but for whatever reason I could not get my spirit together around him. So, we separated and went our separate ways.

At that moment I just knew God was about to take me through a process. I begin to think about if only I had received advice on how to love myself, not accept any everything, walk in confidence, and the truth about my mate will arrive in God's timing. So, I decided to refocus and work on myself. I begin to read the word more and

I NEVER GOT

not just when I felt led to open the book but daily. I begin to align myself up with the people, places, and things that would help me grow. Yes, it was hard, but I never gave up. By staying focused and making this a daily lifestyle this had started to become my normal routine. Speaking positive affirmations over myself; I would constantly tell myself I am more than enough. I shall be in position. I will not be unaware of my value any longer, yet appreciate who I am, and who I am becoming. This begin to shape me. Erasing those negative words, thoughts, and the perspective of how saw things.

Here I am today a single, intelligent, fearfully and wonderfully made woman of God walking in my purpose to help other young ladies and women love themselves, value, accept, and to recognize she is enough. Teaching her that settling and latching on to ever guy that comes by is not of you. You are loved and you shall now be able to look in the mirror and say so.

My advice to you is no matter what has happened in the past, it did not define you. Just like my excitement with tying my shoes for the first and succeed you can too. Keep trying and never give up. Your success awaits you in every task that you put forth effort to accomplish.

You are

not alone.

Marilyn Elizabeth Porter "M.E." is a woman confidently and intentionally living her purpose - bringing light and wisdom to the world. She makes no apologies for being a woman of unflappable faith and allows her Christianity to shine bright in every arena. And although there are many titles and descriptions that fit her - *Mommy* - is one her most prized accolades. Her God and her children (in that order) have been the driving forces in her life.

You may know her as:
The Soul Shifter - and that she is!

THE BEST ADVICE

The Scatter-Brained Genius' Coach - and that she is! You maybe just beginning to know her as;
The P.U.SH. Strategist - and she is that too!

Marilyn Elizabeth "M.E." is a Kingdom Kid, with a love for business (the marketplace) and marketing and is this perfect combination that allows her to be a blessing to the people is many ways.

She was awarded *The Presidential Lifetime Achievement Award for Volunteer Service under President Barak Hussein Obama;* this honor was coupled with the *Certificate of Congressional Recognition signed by Congressman and Civil Rights Leader John Lewis.*

Dr. Porter is not only an 12 time Bestselling author - one of which includes her own life story "The Pieces of ME (And YOU): An Autobiographical Journal" - she is also a Bestselling Publisher and is a published of contributor The Huffington Post. Most recently, she is one of the co-founders of The Christian Literary Arts Awards.

M.E. Porter is also the founder and pastor of The Pink Pulpit Crusade International - an evangelistic organization with a great mission of spreading God's love throughout the entire world. The PPIC also is committed to Bible teaching and ministry training for women globally.

M.E. proudly holds a BS in Psychology, MS in Leadership Development and an Honorary Doctorate in Ministry Development.

Phenomenal Child of God. A Phenomenal Mother. A Phenomenal Friend. A Phenomenal Business Woman. A Phenomenal Preacher of the Gospel. A Phenomenal Author and Publisher. A Phenomenal Wife (husband not accounted for yet). A Phenomenal Life, Business and Personal Development Coach and Consultant. A Phenomenal Mentor.

Dr. Porter is simply a PHENOMENAL WOMEN!

11. Begin with The End

This is a simple, yet valuable piece of wisdom my dears. Over your lifetime you will have millions, likely billions or trillions of thought processes – and most of them won't be worth thinking all the way threw – throw those in the trash (seriously) – but the ones that are your absolute GENIUS coming to life, think those *allllllllll* the way through to the end, and then go back and create the steps that lead to that final step.

This is how you create an intentional thought life! Yes, you can develop and maintain a thought life of intention – and it begins with training your thoughts to line up with your intended goal. **Random thinking will create random results!** You were designed with God's best intention, and your presence and purpose here on Earth are all very much on purpose in the mind.

Let's look at Jeremiah 29:11;

I NEVER GOT

For I know the plans I have for you"- [this is] the Lord's declaration-"plans for [your] welfare, not for disaster, to give you a future and a hope. (HSBC)

How is it that God already knows that plans for your life – even the parts that you have not lived? Hmmmm...
It's because God started at the end with you – He established your whole life – and then allowed you to be conceived in your mother's womb! YES Girl! God is intentional. God knew who your parents would be – He knew the exact, precise DNA that would be required to create the awesomeness that is YOU! Isn't that amazing?!

I have never been a good math student – in fact I hate it! It makes me nauseous. But as a college student, you will encounter math a class or two, depending on your major, maybe even three – but let me get back to the point. So, I had to pass an Algebra class to graduate and I was in an all-out uproar! Until I found a math tutor that taught me backwards! Yes, he would give me the answers and then challenge me to create the steps that were needed to achieve that answer. Guess what? Knowing the answer and then walking out the steps worked! I earned an A in that class!

THE BEST ADVICE

Now, I am not saying that you will always have the answer given to you first, but what I am telling you is that you should always allow yourself permission to receive the answer, thought or idea and then go back to establish the how. It's okay to begin at the end.

I had a business mentor that also taught me to begin at the end. One of the greatest things that has happened to me because of this method, I no longer get stuck in the process of beginning because I already know there is fantastic reward at the end. I started there, and I have already processed through to the end! I know it's going to be good. I know it will work! And I know that I can do it or find someone who can.

Beginning at the end is such a confidence builder – you already know that you cannot be stopped!

I have had others try to rain on my parade and tell me what I could not do – but I had already seen myself accomplishing the very thing that they are telling me won't work! ***Beginning at the end gives you vision!***

Let's take a trip to the end, concerning your life;
I SEE YOU loved.
I SEE YOU healed.
I SEE YOU joy-filled.

I SEE YOU wealthy.

I SEE YOU wise.

I SEE YOU whole and complete.

I SEE YOU successful in all things.

I SEE YOU serving others.

I SEE YOU! Can you see you? Open your eyes up to YOU! I want you to see yourself as your future self as the best possible version of YOU. You see? Good! Now come on back to today and begin taking the steps that will get you to that intended end!

Your mission, if you wish to accept it:

(please initial your choice)

I accept _____

I refuse _____

Go out into the world and do everything in your power (which is the power of God in you – and you can do all things through Christ that is in you Phil. 4:13) to become what you SEE as your God ordained end.

THE BEST ADVICE

You got this!

I NEVER GOT

Here are other suggested titles written and complied by Marilyn E Porter:

- *HERSTORY Reveals His Glory*
- *The Pieces of ME (And YOU)*
- *Stories from The Pink Pulpit – Women in Ministry Speak*

Available on Amazon

or

www.thescatterbrainedgenius.com

Dr. Porter is available for speaking engagements in the following capacities; keynote, panel member, breakout sessions and facilitator – in both the corporate sector and the faith-based community.

Business Phone: 470-729-1212

Email Contact: info@thescatterbrainedgenius.com

Facebook: www.facebook.com/coachmarilyneporter

www.ingramcontent.com/pod-product-compliance
Lightning Source LLC
Chambersburg PA
CBHW071209070526
44584CB00019B/2972